Season of Renewal

A Diary for Women Moving Beyond the Loss of a Love

Judith Finlayson

Crown Publishers, Inc. New York

Published by Crown Publishers, Inc., 201 East 50th Street, New York, New York 10022. Member of the Crown Publishing Group.

Random House, Inc. New York, Toronto, London, Sydney, Auckland

CROWN is a trademark of Crown Publishers, Inc.

Manufactured in the United States of America

ISBN 0-517-59249-5

10 9 8 7 6 5 4 3 2 1

First Edition

Contents

"Life, believe, is not a dream
So dark as sages say;
Oft a little morning rain
Foretells a pleasant day."

CHARLOTTE BRONTË, 1846

Introduction

*S*eparating from someone you love is one of life's most painful experiences, and yet it is a circumstance that most people endure at some point in their lives, often more than once. Even so, there are few rituals or formal means of support to help people through this agonizing time.

I began to keep a journal when my first husband and I were divorcing, more than fifteen years ago. That experience taught me that journal keeping can be a priceless tool for encouraging a broken heart to mend. At its most basic, writing in a diary is an investment in yourself— a statement of self-value at a time when feelings of failure and worthlessness are likely to be prominent.

In recent years, a number of writers and psychotherapists have begun to explore new frontiers of journal keeping, defining the diary as a powerful tool for generating personal growth. But when I began to keep my journal, I was unaware of these developments. More than anything else, I felt an urge to discover who I was.

Although my separation from my husband was civilized, as such things go, by the time the "sold" sign went up on the house we had so carefully renovated, I felt as if I'd been hit by a bus. In addition to leaving my marriage, I had decided to change careers, moving from the editorial side of book and magazine publishing to the precarious profession of "freelance writer." Suddenly, all the things I had relied on for my identity were gone: my beautiful house, my handsome husband, even my career. I wasn't sure there was anything left to call "me."

But I did know that I wanted to find out who this person might be if, in fact, she existed. I also felt a powerful urge to spend some time alone, away from the distractions of city life, so it seemed that fate was on my side when, by incredible happenstance, I was able to rent a charming house in the country. It was a tiny place, perfect for one, and suitably isolated down a quiet dusty road.

I spent four months in this sanctuary, cultivating my solitude. I didn't know a soul in the area, but hoped that my two personable dogs and a substantial pile of books would pass muster for companionship. Except for the occasional visitor, we were completely alone, without stereo, radio, or TV. Weekly trips into town for supplies and the weekend papers were the full extent of our social life.

I spent a lot of time that summer reading books by women writers I admired. What these women shared, and what I aspired to, was a desire to discover truths about themselves, and the society they inhabited, even if the process proved difficult. Since the themes of their books often dovetailed with my motivations for keeping a journal, it's not surprising that my reading became part of my recorded history.

My diary from that summer is fascinating to me now—not only for what it reveals about myself, but also for its links with the form this journal takes. Obviously, the idea has been gestating for many years. Late into the night, curled up in front of a glowing fire, I would write, intermingling my long outpourings of emotional pain with quotations from the books I was reading.

With hindsight, I can see that I created my own form of psychotherapy, one that particularly suited my situation and my needs. At that point I had an urgent need to document my suffering, to record my emotions over and over again until they were fully expelled. At the same time, in tiny but determined steps, I was moving forward, away from my anguish. I didn't realize it at the time, but when my world collapsed, I went looking for comfort in a familiar source. As an only child I had learned to substitute books for human companionship, so trying to mend the broken wing of my identity, it was easy to fall back on old habits.

Nowadays there's a word that describes the process of using books to heal emotional wounds—bibliotherapy. At its simplest, literature helps people who are hurting to recognize that they are not alone. Moreover, by establishing emotional connections to other people's experience it encourages us to observe ourselves from fresh perspectives. Seeing aspects of our lives that are similar to, but different from, our own experience, distances us from our pain without securing our connections to its emotional reality. These ideas have laid much of the groundwork for this diary.

When I began to keep my journal, I was also unaware of the long tradition of women as journal keepers. Since then, working as a writer who has spent many years charting the emotional lives of women, I've read hundreds of diaries kept by women. Over the years, I've become convinced that diaries provide a unique source of truth about the reality of women's lives. All too often, women's feelings have been at odds with society's views of our proper place and diaries have been a consistent confidant. Documenting and exploring your feelings throughout this time of mourning makes you a member of a distinguished group.

"I want my book to be about love," wrote Elizabeth Smart in her journal in 1939. In 1945 she published her masterpiece, *By Grand Central Station I Sat Down and Wept*, an agonizing account of a young woman's love affair with a married man. In writing the book, she transformed her excruciating pain into art.

While you may not produce a masterpiece, separating from a lover can provide similar opportunities for creativity and growth. The end of a relationship is, in itself, the beginning of a new phase of existence. By compelling you toward introspection, the grieving process can help you to develop valuable insights into yourself and your relationships with others.

As T. S. Eliot observed in *The Cocktail Party*,

Most of the time we take ourselves for granted,
As we have to and live on a little knowledge
About ourselves as we were.

Keeping a diary means that you are no longer taking yourself for granted. You are making a commitment to learning more about yourself. Living an examined life can help you to discover the power buried deep within yourself, power that I believe all of us have, if only we can find it.

In your journey toward self-awareness, you must also learn to make peace with your pain. You have suffered a serious loss. Not only is it normal to be hurting, it would be detrimental if you weren't. So trust your pain. It is a healthy symptom.

Listening to your pain is the first step toward healing. If you don't communicate with your suffering, you will never understand it. And you will pay a serious penalty, perhaps not now, but in the years to come, as unresolved grief can haunt you for the rest of your life.

Working through this diary will help you to move beyond your pain. If you have a supportive therapist to help you through this difficult time, keeping a diary can expedite the healing you generate together. Use your diary to reflect more deeply on issues that have surfaced in therapy, or as a kind of research lab, a place to develop thoughts and ideas that you bring to your therapist for further discussion. This technique was often used by the diarist Anaïs Nin, who frequently refers to cross-pollination between the issues she was simultaneously exploring in therapy and in her diary.

Many people find that keeping a journal is the only therapy they need, but some situations are so painful they may require professional help to heal. Keeping a diary can help you to identify whether or not your problems fall into this category. If you notice repetitive behavior that is hurtful, if you are drinking excessively, using drugs to dull the pain, or contemplating suicide, you should seek professional help immediately.

As you work through your diary, please remember a thought that is fundamental to healing: The simple act of naming your feelings is very empowering. Separation from someone you have loved, or may still love, is a major rite of passage. By providing a place where you can record your deepest emotions, your diary will begin to take on a life of its own. Respect that life and allow it to guide you. Its power will help you to find your true self, the person who is often hidden behind the conflicts and confusions of daily life.

How to Use This Book

Your diary consists of four parts: a working journal, where you can document your relationship in all its complexity; blank pages to reflect upon what you have written; a section to record your dreams; and a reading list of books I hope you will find helpful.

The working section of your journal consists of a series of inquiries into yourself, your former partner, and the nature of your relationship. Many of these are enhanced by affirmations to help get you started in a new direction. Quotations from literature that reflect feelings relevant to separating from a lover are also scattered throughout this section. It may help you to know that your grief will take place in four basic phases: shock (or disbelief), grief (or guilt), rage, and, finally, acceptance or the ability to move on to the next stage of your life. In general terms, the quotations reflect this movement toward self-reliance.

Many people avoid examining their lives because they don't know where to begin. If you're one of those people, the text will help to get you started as a journal writer. Even if you feel comfortable with self-examination, the thoughts you encounter here may inspire you to explore aspects of yourself and your relationship that might not have occurred to you. If some seem startlingly obvious, they are deliberately so. Like the slow, mechanical motion of the act of writing, documenting the concrete details of your relationship should ease you into a state of relaxation that puts you in closer touch with your unconscious and its guidance from within.

Some years ago, I did a workshop with Dr. Ira Progoff, a psychologist who uses journal keeping as a tool for helping people to see the meaning of their lives. Dr. Progoff provides participants with workbooks containing twenty-one color-coded dividers, delineating categories in "dimensions" such as dialogue, depth, and time. Although they may seem cumbersome, the sections have a definite purpose. On one level, Dr. Progoff believes that the mundane act of cataloging the content of our lives make us less self-conscious of our search for ultimate meaning.

In other words, it's easier to see the larger picture of our lives when we aren't aware of looking for it. Documenting the numerous tiny details that characterize your relationship will allow the larger picture to emerge, much like the process an artist goes through in constructing a painting.

Don't feel obligated to do all of the investigations or to examine all the issues they raise. As I mentioned, they are really designed to get you started. You will know intuitively which ones are right for you. In fact, you may not see the relevance of a particular investigation until much later in the process of keeping your diary. In that case, return and do it then.

If you feel the need to write more than the space allows, by all means do so. Keep a blank page book for this purpose or write on loose pages and fold them into your journal, which is what I often do when I feel the need to write and don't have my journal with me.

The quotations build upon and expand the process of self-analysis begun with the investigations. As any book lover knows, well-crafted words are an effective means of evoking emotion. In fact, as Franz Kafka reflected, "A book should serve as an axe for the frozen sea within us." Although they might not mirror your emotions exactly, these thoughts will help you to tap into other people's feelings and equate them with your own. Situating your individual pain within the continuum of human experience will encourage you to grow beyond your current problems, however devastating they might be.

Any situation can be seen from many different points of view. In fact, telling the same story from the perspective of different characters is a device that novelists have used, often to great effect. This technique can help you to maximize the benefit of journal keeping. Looking at your relationship from many points of view, including those represented by other people's thoughts, can help you to understand it more completely. As you identify common themes that cut across various aspects of your life, you'll begin to see direction and meaning in your experience.

The Dream Journal provides a place to record your significant dreams as a record of self-discovery. Dreams have been defined as a road map to the unconscious, a source of unique information about ourselves. Documenting the content of our dreams helps us to understand what they are trying to tell us about our lives.

Your diary also consists of blank pages for Reflections. These pages exist so that you can revisit earlier thoughts and feelings. Looking back and reflecting on what you have written is one of the most beneficial aspects of keeping a diary. And, if you read carefully, you should begin to see patterns in your life that can reveal areas of weakness requiring change or sources of inner strength.

The final pages contain a Reading List. The books included focus on issues of self-reliance and self-knowledge, as well as separation from a lover. I have also included some books on journal keeping. All of the selections have said something meaningful to me, or they have made me laugh. I have chosen them carefully, based on my perception of their value to someone experiencing loss and a desire for growth, but they very much reflect my own tastes in literature and psychology and if you don't find them helpful, I am totally to blame.

Before you begin to work in your diary, please remember that emotional work is every bit as tiring as hard physical labor, so set aside plenty of time, find a quiet spot, and make yourself comfortable. Go with the flow and don't force yourself to do too much at once. Write what is bubbling up inside you, what your heart needs to know.

In some ways, keeping a journal requires a quantum leap in understanding. You must learn to think of your inner life as a precious asset that needs to be carefully maintained. This perception is particularly difficult for women since our value has traditionally been tied to the work we do for others, often at great cost to ourselves.

Try to visualize the writing that you do in your diary as an investment in yourself. Think of this book as an emotional bank account where compound interest is accruing. As with a high-performance mutual fund, the effort you make today will pay substantial dividends in the years to come.

Anatomy of a Relationship

This investigation will help you to focus on specific aspects of your relationship. By identifying problem areas in your past unions, you are less likely to make similar misjudgments in the future. As you document one aspect of your relationship, you may find your mind wandering down new avenues of thought. Follow these directions and see where they lead. This is your unconscious guiding you, and it will help you to get where you need to go.

Completing this investigation will provide you with a thumbnail sketch of your relationship, one that can serve as a starting point for deeper examination.

The Beginning

Like a Rorschach or inkblot test, the beginning of a relationship can be read for clues to its eventual demise. Think about how and where you met, what you remember about your lover, and what you particularly liked and disliked. Then move on to significant memories of your first date and falling in love.

Consider your intuition, whether it was working well or if it was shut down for some reason which may only become obvious in the fullness of time.

I became involved in this relationship because
it fulfilled some need. I am trying to identify my motivations
so I will not make the same mistakes again.

"No, it wasn't death she was afraid of. It was this life of hers that was beginning to remind her of that gray intensive care waiting room."

FANNIE FLAGG, 1988

Socializing

Since every couple exists as part of a larger community, you may find it helpful to consider the friends you had as a twosome. Who were they, yours or your partner's, or were they equally shared? Many people lead interesting, exciting lives as single people, but when they become part of a couple, they soon become so focused on doing things as a team that they lose contact with their old network of friends and activities. If this happened to you, reflect on why this was so and what it says about your relationship. Also, think about what happened to your "couple" friendships since your relationship ended, as traditional wisdom assumes that they will follow the more powerful partner.

Friends are a valuable resource. I must choose my friends carefully
to help me through this difficult time.

*"I stopped washing my hair.
It did not seem possible
to stand under the shower
and come out feeling alive
and new. It did not seem
worthwhile even to try."*
SALLIE BINGHAM, 1976

Being Together

Studies show that one partner in a relationship usually makes more concessions and adjustments to the other's personality, values, and life-style. Consider your day-to-day life with this in mind. Who invested the most in the relationship? Identify the best of times and the worst of times in your relationship and think about why this was so.

I deserve to be in a relationship with someone
who cares about meeting my needs.

"Who shuffles by me gripping chairs for support? I do.... I am without words. I am without thoughts.... I am dying for love."

ELIZABETH SMART, 1945

Working

The pressures of work can create serious stresses in a relationship. People are often tense or tired at the end of a work day and this can threaten intimacy, not only with your partner but also with yourself. Reflect on the importance of work to you and your partner, and whether or not it ever interfered with your relationship. Did either one of you use work addictively to keep you from confronting personal problems? Did your partner support your work and recognize its value (this includes unpaid work in the home)? If you and your partner lived together, concentrate for a few moments on the sharing of domestic work, your feelings toward your partner's efforts as a housemate and, if relevant, as a parent.

I must remember that I made an important contribution
to this relationship and that my work in all its facets
needs to be acknowledged.

"*There are two marriages,
then, in every marital union,
his and hers. And his...
is better than hers.*"
JESSIE BERNARD, 1972

Managing Money

In our society, money is at least as likely as love to make the world go 'round. Finances can be problematic in any relationship, since money often represents a battleground where more complicated battles are fought. Were hidden money motivations an issue in your relationship? Did either of you have difficulty managing money? If you have children, think about whether you were prepared for the financial burdens they represented and if this affected your relationship. If separation will affect your financial status, explore your feelings and fears.

I must be realistic about my finances and not allow irrational

attitudes toward money to get in the way of my healing.

> *"At the end of my first year of marriage, I realized that if I wanted a peaceful home and I did—I would simply have to become more submissive, although it was not my nature to do so."*
> AURELIA SCHOBER PLATH,
> 1975

Making Love

Balancing the seesaw of emotional, intellectual, and erotic interest is a very delicate task. Many people believe that sexual desire wanes as commitment grows, that the warmth and security represented by the couple are at odds with the fire of passion. If one partner has been unfaithful, the perceived betrayal can be shattering to the other. Think about your relationship with these thoughts in mind.

My sexuality is too precious to be
wasted on meaningless affairs.

"It is a common story, I know. Passion choked by domesticity. Or one might say that we married in haste and repented at leisure."

MARGARET DRABBLE, 1964

Coming Apart

Changes in a relationship don't arrive suddenly. Clues accumulate gradually, over a period of time, until we can no longer deny the end is near. Can you identify early signs that your relationship might not last forever? When did you know for sure that it was over? Focus on that moment. Try to understand what you were most afraid of and assess how far you have moved beyond this state.

I must understand my past before
I can get on with my future.

"I kept my voice low. I was asking because I was my mother's daughter and I was supposed to be courageous and honest. I didn't want an honest answer. I wished for him to deny everything, or to hand me any contrived explanation."

MAYA ANGELOU, 1981

Preparing for the Future

Visualizing a positive future is an important step in moving toward it. Concentrate on your hopes and dreams. Imagine yourself a stronger, more self-aware person. Document the steps you have taken to make this person a reality. This includes the decision to keep this journal. Think about other things you might do to merge this happier, healthier person with your current self.

I deserve to be happy.

"Nothing is so good as it seems beforehand."
GEORGE ELIOT, 1861

Our Relationship Contract

All relationships are based on various kinds of contracts between the partners. Sometimes these contracts are formal, written documents that provide for specific details such as financial obligations, whether or not the couple intends to have children, and the division of property if the relationship ends. But even when a couple carefully itemizes such details, their "contract" also involves a set of unspoken expectations. Successful enduring relationships result when these conscious and unconscious expectations are adequately fulfilled by both partners. They also depend upon a couple's ability to rewrite their contract to meet changing needs.

The following investigation can help you to identify the nature of your contract with your partner and why it ceased to apply. Documenting the contractual aspects of your relationship and then comparing your thoughts to what you wrote in Investigation One may help you to identify pressure points in your relationship that have deeper implications.

Expectations

All of us came of age with incredible expectations of romantic love, from Fred Astaire and Ginger Rogers sipping champagne and dancing till dawn, to the more basic approach represented by "Me Tarzan, you Jane." These images influence the way we experience our intimate relationships. When the person we love fails to live up to our expectations, it is easy to feel that we have been deceived. However, it's equally possible that we were swept away by our own dreams of romantic love.

If your lover failed to live up to your expectations, think about whether you were misled or if you misled yourself. Speculate on what your partner's expectations were of you and whether or not you fulfilled them. (Consider things such as financial stability and social status as well as love and happiness.)

_I will try to become a more complete person who will look
for someone to share my life, not fulfill my needs._

"True love is the rarest
of all emotions and one that
has been conspicuous only by
its absence ever since mankind
dropped from the trees."
JILL TWEEDIE, 1979

"A man's home may be seen to be his castle on the outside; inside it is more often his nursery."

CLARE BOOTHE LUCE, 1974

"This was the painful thing: that she had been so wrong about him. That she was capable once of such abject self-deception. Or still is, because in some way she still misses him; him, or her own mistaken adoration."
MARGARET ATWOOD, 1991

Compatibility

Getting along together—enjoying the same movies, sharing the same values, and having complementary goals—is an important component of lasting and fulfilling relationships. Since the romantic tradition suggests that love will conquer all, it's easy to ignore these practical realities.

The truth is, some couples are totally mismatched because they have been attracted to each other by deep (and largely unconscious needs). These relationships can be long-lasting, but they are characterized by constant conflict.

Take a look at your relationship from the point of view of compatibility. Did you share similar values, interests, and goals? Were you and your partner happy to begin with or was your relationship always conflicted? If abuse—physical or emotional—figured in your relationship, think about it here.

_____

_____

_____

_____

_____

_____

_____

_____

_____

_____

_____

_____

_____

_____

_____

_____

_____

_____

_____

_____

When I am ready to become involved again,
I will look for someone who will be
a good companion as well as a lover.

"No one can build his security
upon the nobleness of
another person."
WILLA CATHER, 1912

"If men could see us as we really are, they would be a little amazed; but the cleverest, the acutest men are often under an illusion about women: they do not read them in a true light: they misapprehend them, both for good and evil."
CHARLOTTE BRONTË, 1849

Personal Growth

With the passage of time, most of us acquire wisdom and develop as individuals, but we rarely, if ever, do this totally in synch with the other important people in our lives. Different rates of growth is one of the most common reasons for relationship breakdown. When both partners grow as individuals, even in different directions, their relationship can continue to work. But when one grows and the other doesn't, the balance is thrown out of whack. Couples can enjoy a long period of happiness only to discover, with the passage of time, they have nothing in common.

Think about the rate of growth you and your partner were experiencing and the directions you took. Reflect on the influence this may have had on your relationship.

Through slow but steady growth
I can become the person I want to be.

"Female, a Quixote is no Quixote at all; told about a woman, the tale of being caught in a fantasy becomes the story of everyday life."
RACHEL BROWNSTEIN, 1982

"*What it is, I guess,*
is that I don't really miss him.
I miss something that must
have been us."
LOIS GOULD, 1970

"'No, Burt, I never really liked you,' a surprised, rude little voice said inside me. 'I married you because I wanted to be married and I wanted children. The ring, the bed, the security. But you I never really liked. And I suspect the same may be true on your side. It's just habit or inertia or cowardice that's kept us together all this time.'"
CONSTANCE BERESFORD-HOWE, 1973

My Past, My Present, and My Future

$\mathcal{E}$very stage of our emotional lives has been shaped by our previous experience. Similarly, how we deal with the present affects our future. Because we have a natural inclination to cling to familiar emotions, even when they aren't good for us, we should periodically look back on our lives to see if unhealthy patterns of behavior are undermining our current success.

At a conscious level, most people make a commitment to another person because they are "in love" and they feel that being with that person will make them happy. But all of us bring a complex collection of emotions and inner conflicts to any relationship and many of the emotional needs we look toward a romantic partner to fulfill are deeply rooted in our family relationships.

This investigation will help you to see your relationship with your partner against the backdrop of all the other significant relationships in your life. It may also help you to identify patterns in your behavior that you might want to change.

My Parenting Figures

～

Our childhood experiences made us the adults we are today. Family values, the backgrounds of our parenting figures, how we were disciplined, and all the other factors that comprise the texture of family life, influenced the kind of person we became. Think about the essential features of your relationship with your parenting figures—the same sex and the opposite sex—and how that shows up in your attitudes and behavior. What makes you feel good about these relationships? What makes you feel sad?

By understanding both the good and the bad parts of
my upbringing, I will become a stronger, wiser person.

"Great are the penalties
of those who dare
resist the behests of the
tyrant custom."
ELIZABETH CADY
STANTON, 1898

"The present enshrines the past."
SIMONE DE BEAUVOIR,
1949

"Nobody who has not been in the interior of a family can say what the difficulties of any individual of that family may be."

Jane Austen, 1815

My Love
Relationship(s)

The roles and patterns of behavior we learned in our families affect the qualities we look for in a mate. Many psychotherapists and relationship counselors have noted the extraordinary "sixth sense" that people bring to falling in love, how strongly they are attracted to people who reflect their own conflicts in both positive and negative ways. As the French writer Colette once reflected, "The infatuation of a girl in love is neither as constant nor as blind as she tries to believe." Think about your relationship with your partner in this context. What aspects are similar to the relationship that your parenting figures had? In what ways did your relationship differ? Think about other rela-tionships you've had. Can you identify any patterns?

The roots of my relationship and its failure
extend far beyond myself.

"A man is very revealed by his wife, just as a woman is revealed by her husband. People never marry beneath or above themselves, I assure you."

CAROL MATTHAU, 1992

"It was good. And nothing good is ever lost. It stays part of a person, becomes part of one's character."

ROSAMUNDE PILCHER, 1987

My Desire to Please

The desire to please our parents is normal. So, too, the inclination to rebel. Not surprisingly, these motivations often find an outlet in the selection of a mate. Consider your relationship with your partner within this context. Was your relationship with your partner approved by significant people in you life— friends, parents, siblings, and other relatives? Why or why not? Think about your motivation in gaining or rejecting this approval. Did this have any bearing on the breakdown of your relationship?

_Cleaning up the unfinished business in my life will help
me to face my future with confidence._

"What a wonderful faculty is memory!—the most mysterious and inexplicable in the great riddle of life."
SUSANNA MOODIE, 1853

With or Without Children

Most of us associate our image of the couple with children. Like it or not, the kind of family life portrayed in "Leave It to Beaver" has influenced our dreams, even if it no longer reflects statistical reality. This means that women who haven't had children, by choice or by chance, can find that their absence colors their feelings about themselves.

Women with children have different concerns. In its own way, having a baby creates as much of a crisis, a transition from one stage of life to another, as the end of a relationship. Although many people experience the birth of a baby as the beginning of a family, for some it is more vividly remembered as the loss of a twosome.

Whether or not you have had children—even if they were inappropriate to your relationship—you may find it useful to look at your relationship from some of the following perspectives.

Being Pregnant

Even today, when women exercise considerable control over our reproductive choices, pregnancy and ambivalence are likely to go hand in hand. Becoming a parent is a major rite of passage, so not surprisingly, pregnancy can easily become a focal point for other conflicts within a relationship. Consider these thoughts and your own feelings about being pregnant. Was your partner happy or dismayed to learn you were having a baby? Was this a time of closeness or distancing between you? If you have more than one child, try to think about the differences and similarities in all your pregnancies.

"Handfuls of babies, that is what you are really in need of.... Then as the father of a family, he cannot leave you. Think of his delight and excitement when he saw you."
KATHERINE MANSFIELD,
1911

Not Being Pregnant

Since women's roles have traditionally been associated with caring for children, women who are infertile or who have chosen not to have children can often feel inadequate. If it is applicable to do so, think about how not having children may have affected your relationship, both positively and negatively. If you ever terminated a pregnancy or miscarried, reflect on the impact this may have had on you and your relationship.

"She had thought then that there are a few things no one ever tells women. She supposed it wasn't a conspiracy; maybe it was a kindness. When she was pregnant the first time, a few people had at least suggested some of the possibilities. Martin's mother had told her that her life would never again be the same, not altogether in a congratulatory tone."

ROBB FORMAN DEW, 1992

Body Image

For some women pregnancy functions as a blatant symbol of their sexuality and their transition into the role of woman. Other women view it simply as a means to the end of having a baby. And still others find the idea of being pregnant physically repulsive. Reflect on how you feel about your body. If you have children, did you enjoy being pregnant? Did it make you feel feminine and vital or did you feel heavy and fat? Whether or not you have been pregnant, think about what makes you feel attractive and what your partner found most desirable about you. How did this fit with your own feelings about yourself?

"Every natural tendency
to self-indulgence is steadily
increased by the life service
of an entire wife."
CHARLOTTE PERKINS
GILMAN, 1903

Responsibility

To some extent, everyone is ambivalent about parenthood: It's an awesome responsibility. If you are a parent, think about how your partner accepted the additional responsibility of children. Was caring for the children your job or a shared responsibility? If you aren't a parent, think about your feelings toward responsibility in more general terms. Was your partner there for you when you needed support? How did this affect your relationship?

"After marriage all things change. And one of them better be you."
ELIZABETH HAWES, 1948

Independence

Traditionally, "femininity" has been associated with dependence on others for one's sense of self. Consider the role that independence—or its lack—has played in your own self-concept. If you are a parent, you might want to think about these feelings in regard to your children. Did you feel that you lost your independence after your first child was born, and if so, did this bother you? Or, perhaps, you felt powerful for the first time in your life?

"She was thirty-nine.... No she did not envy her eighteen-year-old self at all. But she did envy, envied every day more bitterly, that young girl's genuine independence, large-ness, scope and courage."

DORIS LESSING, 1958

Children from Other Relationships

The "blended family" is an increasingly common phenom-
enon and one that comes with its own unique set of stresses and
strains. Did either you or your partner have a child or children
from a previous relationship? If so, think about the effect this had
on your relationship.

> *"I have a very clear, keen memory of myself the day after I was married: I was sweeping a floor."*
> ADRIENNE RICH, 1976

Personal Inventory

If you were going to the bank to borrow money for a new venture, they would demand that you prepare a business plan—a statement of your assets and liabilities, as well as the feasibility of your future success. Zeroing in on your personal capital and identifying your long-term goals lay the foundation for a successful venture. The business of your life can benefit from a similar analysis.

Assets and Liabilities

Make a list of all your assets and liabilities. Things you might think about include:

- *financial*
- *skills and abilities*
- *intelligence*
- *interests and hobbies*
- *professional qualifications*
- *physical health*
- *emotional well-being*

- *personality*
- *friends*
- *life-style*
- *home*
- *networks (both professional and personal)*
- *self-sufficiency*
- *dreams and goals*

Reflect on what this list says about you. Decide which areas you want to strengthen and set definite objectives and time frames for shoring them up. Think about ways that you can use your assets to better advantage. Get a friend to help you with this, if you wish.

"All this, if one could regard
it rationally, came down
to a few readjustments in one's
menage and a slight
social awkwardness which one
would soon outgrow."
ELIZABETH BOWEN, C. 1920

Myself as
a Social Being

The nature of the grieving process means that you will often feel that you don't have the energy to see people or go out. Although these emotions have an important role to play in the process of introspection, it is critical to your well-being that you make an effort to balance these feelings by socializing with people and engaging in activities outside yourself.

Make a list of all your friends and family members whose company you enjoy. Make another list of the things that you like to do that don't require your partner. Include new activities and skills such as taking up a sport or becoming involved in a hobby. Promise yourself that at least once a week you will undertake one new thing that you want to do, and that you will spend time with someone who makes you laugh.

> "Miranda was already completely unlike any friend Emmy had ever had. If it had not been for the awful isolation into which she had suddenly been plunged, she would not have dreamed of knowing her."
>
> ALISON LURIE, 1962

"The loneliest man in literature has a wife whose loneliness is not even noticed, least of all by herself."

CAROLYN G. HEILBRUN, 1979

Things That Make Me Happy

Too often we see the cup as half empty rather than half full. By documenting things that make you happy, you can create a resource in this journal that you can revisit when you need cheering up. Return to this list and add to it as you identify more sources of joy.

*"It has been the longest
time since she had a rib-
scraping laugh. She had
forgotten how deep and
down it could be."*
Toni Morrison, 1985

My Perfect Future

Under a separate heading, write your wish list for the future. This is slightly different from identifying things that make you happy. It is kind of a mission statement of what you want to accomplish. You may be surprised at how helpful it can be to articulate your goals. Include in this section any plans for the future that you had years ago but set aside for various reasons. Now might be the perfect time to revise them.

"We may emerge
from times of traumatic
worthlessness and
low self-esteem with an
increased immunity to
similar assaults, a stronger
sense of ourselves, and a
better defense against
future challenges."
GLORIA STEINEM, 1992

"One needs something to believe in, something for which one can have whole-hearted enthusiasm. One needs to feel that one's life had meaning, that one is needed in this world."
HANNAH SENESH, 1938

"The deepest responsibility
of each of us is to become
more fully who we are, to
live closer to the truth."
RAM DASS AND
MIRABAI BUSH, 1992

Looking at
My Love

*U*sing information from the investigations you have completed, create a portrait of your former love. On one level, this sketch of your partner's dominant characteristics will help you to understand what you saw in this person. On another, it will help you to define your partner as an individual separate from you. If you are feeling particularly negative, give yourself permission to focus on your partner's defects. The important thing now is not to be fair to your partner—you can do that after you have put this experience behind you—but rather to purge yourself of emotions you need to get rid of so that you can get on with the business of your life.

"When I was in college,
I had a list of what I
wanted in a husband. A
long list... Then I grew up
and settled for a low-grade
lunatic who kept hamsters."
NORA EPHRON, 1983

*"My true friends
have always given me
that supreme proof of
devotion, a spontaneous
aversion for the man
I loved."*
COLETTE, 1928

*"With a flash of insight
that freed her forever, she saw...
the price each [woman]
had paid with whom he had
been intimate either in love or
friendship, in being obliged
to shut off, in order to meet him
in his world...three-fourths
of their being."*

DOROTHY RICHARDSON, 1938

Exploring

Solitude

A Journal
of Self-Reliance

$\mathcal{U}$se this section of your journal to document the last stage of your journey to a happier more independent self. Enjoy the company of other women who share with you some of the knowledge gained from their own transitions.

"Grief may be joy
misunderstood."
ELIZABETH BARRETT
BROWNING, 1862

159

"That is what is strange—
that friends, even passionate
love, are not my real life
unless there is time alone in
which to discover what is
happening or has happened."
MAY SARTON, 1973

"It isn't pathetic anymore to be single. As a friend of mine had the wit to reply when someone asked if she were married, 'Good God, no, are you?'"
JANE HOWARD, 1973

"I enjoy being alone. I don't tell people this because they'll accuse me of either lying or deluding myself. But I do.... I feel I don't ever want to be involved again.... You see, I have all that I want for now."

PAULA MARSHALL, 1977

"Men are irrelevant. Women are happy or unhappy, fulfilled or unfulfilled, and it has nothing to do with men."
FAYE WELDON, 1971

*"Fortunately, [psycho]-
analysis is not the only
way to resolve inner conflicts.
Life itself still remains a
very effective therapist."*
KAREN HORNEY, 1945

"I realize that when one
no longer loves,
one no longer lives."
GEORGE SAND, 1834

*"I love my past.
I love my present. I'm not
ashamed of what I've had
and I'm not sad because I
have it no longer."*
COLETTE, 1926

Dream Journal

Even after you fall asleep at night, your mind keeps on working. Dreams are the product of its nocturnal efforts. By putting us in touch with unfamiliar areas of our personality, dreams can help us to understand important aspects of ourselves. Writing down the content of our dreams makes them part of our conscious life and helps us to identify the messages they are trying to send us.

This dream journal is a place to record your dreams during the process of separation. Document them by date and refer back to them to see what they reveal about your movement through this important stage of your life.

Reflections

*R*ereading what you have written in your diary is one of its most valuable functions. By reading what you have recorded, you will be able to see the changes in yourself and to identify themes in your life. Sometimes you may find yourself cringing when you read about your past self. I know I often do. But if seeing this person makes you unhappy—especially if it does—you should feel inspired because it means that you have grown beyond her.

Enjoy the story of your life and listen to what it is telling you.

Reading List

The following is a short list of books, both fiction and nonfiction, that should be both interesting and helpful to someone separating from a lover. The list is by no means comprehensive. In fact, it is highly selective, reflecting my own tastes and biases. But these are all books that shed some light on relationships, self-reliance, journal keeping, and/or female psychology. I hope you find them helpful.

Fiction

Margaret Atwood, *Lady Oracle* (Toronto: McClelland & Steward, 1976). An often hilarious novel about a woman who leads several secret lives—as a self-effacing wife, notorious author and adulteress—and who plans her own death in order to avoid exposure.

Colette, *Cheri* and *The Last of Cheri* (New York: Farrar, Straus and Giroux, 1951). Two novels examining an older woman's feelings about her love affair with a younger man and its ending.

Nora Ephron, *Heartburn* (New York: Pocket Books, 1984). A wickedly funny novel about the breakdown of a marriage that proves, as one reviewer claimed, "writing well is the best revenge."

Fannie Flagg, *Fried Green Tomatoes at the Whistle Stop Café,* (New York: McGraw Hill, 1988). A warm and funny novel about women's lives, full of love for its often eccentric characters and hope for the kinds of communities they are able to create.

Erica Jong, *Fear of Flying* (New York: Holt, Rinehart and Winston, 1973). The first best-selling book to explore the liberating element of divorce. Often hilarious and certainly shocking for the time.

John Updike, *Too Far To Go: The Maples Stories* (New York: Fawcett Books, 1979). A collection of touching and sensitive stories charting the decline and fall of a marriage from a man's perspective.

Faye Weldon, *The Life and Loves of a She Devil* (London: Hodder and Stoughton, 1983). A funny and intelligent novel about a downtrodden housewife who, when her husband abandons her for a glamorous writer, refuses to go gently into the dark night of rejection.

Nonfiction

A. Alvarez, *Life After Marriage, Love in an Age of Divorce* (New York: Simon & Schuster, 1981). A personal and cultural meditation on divorce, full of many interesting insights and observations, both contemporary and historical.

Karen Blixen, *Out of Africa* (London: Jonathon Cape Ltd., 1973). A profoundly moving autobiography about loss and the triumph of the human spirit.

Rachel M. Brownstein, *Becoming a Heroine, Reading About Women in Novels* (New York: Penguin Books, 1984). An intriguing examination of how novels have consistently given women the message that marriage is our true vocation.

Dorothy Dinnerstein, *The Mermaid and the Minotaur: Sexual Arrangements and Human Malaise* (New York: Harper and Row, 1976). A provocative and seminal work that argues that women's monopoly of early childcare has disturbing consequences not only for relationships between the sexes, but also for the human race.

Carolyn G. Heilbrun, *Writing, A Woman's Life* (New York: Ballantine Books, 1989). A beautifully written book about women writers and their quest for independence.

Dalma Heyn, *The Erotic Silence of the American Wife* (New York: Turtle Bay Books, 1992). An engrossing look at contemporary marriage and how many women have chosen to cope with its shortcomings by having extra-marital affairs.

Judith Lewis Herman, M.D., *Trauma and Recovery: The Aftermath of Violence from Domestic Abuse to Political Terror* (New York: Basic Books, 1992). Establishing the connections between the traumatic experiences of men in war and women who are victims of assault, battery and other forms of sexual and domestic violence, this book legitimizes the study of trauma as an all-too-common and life-destroying part of ordinary human experience.

Dana Crowley Jack, *Silencing the Self: Women and Depression* (Cambridge, Mass.: Harvard University Press, 1991). A brilliant and often gripping analysis of how women often sacrifice their own needs to remain in relationships and become depressed as a result.

Anne Morrow Lindbergh, *Hour of Gold, Hour of Lead* (New York: Harcourt, Brace, Jovanovich, 1973). Coming to terms with the kidnapping and murder of her baby provides the author with the impetus for parts of this very moving book which vividly portrays the experience of grief and the eventual movement toward a new beginning.

Jane Miller, *Women Writing About Men* (New York: Pantheon Books, 1986). A fascinating book that looks at what women writers have written about men and the relationships between the sexes.

Jean Baker Miller, *Toward a New Psychology of Women* (Boston: Beacon Press, 1977). A milestone in our understanding of female psychology, this small book looks at women's quest for authenticity within the context of meeting others' needs and concludes that women's way of living may have far more to offer the world than traditional wisdom suggests.

Glenda, Riley, *Divorce: An American Tradition* (New York: Oxford University Press, 1991). An often lively and illuminating history of divorce, showing that the ritual enjoys a long and vibrant tradition.

May Sarton, *Journal of a Solitude* (New York: W. W. Norton, 1977). A frank and often painful book about a woman's search for herself during a year she spent living alone.

Gloria Steinem, *Revolution From Within* (Boston: Little, Brown, 1992). A thoughtful and inspiring book examining self-esteem and why it is so difficult to achieve.

Anthony Storr, *Solitude: A Return to the Self* (London: Flamingo, 1989). An examination of the virtues of solitude by an eminent British psychiatrist who challenges the view that happiness is dependent upon success in personal relationships.

Jill Tweedie, *In the Name of Love: Love in Theory and Practice Throughout the Ages* (New York: Pantheon, 1979).

A challenging and often controversial book that examines concepts of love from an historical perspective and concludes that much of what occurs in its name reflects social needs much more than a magic force.

Robert S. Weiss, *Going It Alone: The Family Life and Social Situation of the Single Parent* (New York: Basic Books, 1979). A thorough and often illuminating look at single-parenting by an esteemed professor of sociology.

Journal Keeping

Joanna Field, *A Life of One's Own* (Los Angeles: J. P. Tarcher, Inc., 1981). A woman's reflections on what keeping a journal taught her about the meaning of her life.

Kay Leigh Hagan, *Internal Affairs: A Journal-Keeping Workbook for Self-Intimacy* (San Francisco: Harper & Row, 1990). A "hands-on" guide to using the journal for self-actualization.

Lyn Lifshin (ed.), *Ariadne's Thread: A Collection of Contemporary Women's Journals* (New York: Harper & Row, 1982). A widely ranging collection of journals that provides a unique look into the thoughts and feelings of contemporary women.

Mary Jane Moffat and Charlotte Painter (eds.), *Revelations: Diaries of Women* (New York: Vintage Books, 1975). Selections from women's diaries, interesting for the wide range of experience they capture, as well as their insights into the inner lives of women.

Anaïs Nin, *The Diary of Anaïs Nin*, edited by Gunther Stuhlmann (New York: The Swallow Press and Harcourt, Brace and World, 1966). Although they have been criticized for their self-absorption, Nin's diaries deserve to be read as groundbreakers exploring the diary as a medium for self-analysis.

Ira Progoff, *At a Journal Workshop* (New York: Dialogue House Library, 1977). The basic textbook for using the journal-keeping process developed by Dr. Progoff.

Tristine Rainer, *The New Diary* (Los Angeles: J. P. Tarcher, 1978). A "how-to" book on maximizing the value of journal keeping as a tool for self-analysis.

Acknowledgments

Quotations used throughout the book have been taken from the following sources.

Angelou, Maya, *The Heart of a Woman* (New York: Random House, Inc. 1981). Used by permission of Random House, Inc.

Atwood, Margaret, "The Bog Man," in *Wilderness Tips* (New York: Doubleday and Co., Inc., 1991). Used by permission of the author.

Austen, Jane, *Pride and Prejudice* (London: Penguin Classics, 1985).

Beresford-Howe, Constance, *The Book of Eve* (Toronto: Macmillan of Canada, 1973). Used by permission of Macmillan of Canada.

Bernard, Jessie, *The Future of Marriage* (New Haven: Yale University Press, 1972). Used by permission of Yale University Press.

Bingham, Sallie, "Mending," in *Solo, Women on Woman Alone,* edited by Linda Hamalian and Leo Hamalian (New York: Delacorte Press, 1977). Used by permission of the author.

Bowen, Elizabeth, "Making Arrangements," in *The Collected Stories of Elizabeth Bowen* (New York: Alfred A. Knopf, 1981). Used by permission of the estate of the author, Jonathan Cape Ltd. and Random House, Inc.

Brontë, Charlotte, *Shirley* (Oxford: Oxford University Press, 1979).

Browning, Elizabeth Barrett, "De Profundis" in *Selected Poems of Elizabeth Barrett Browning* (London: Chatto & Windus, 1988).

Brownstein, Rachel, *Becoming a Heroine* (New York: The Viking Press, 1982). Used by permission of Viking Penguin, a division of Penguin Books U.S.A., Inc.

Cather, Willa, *Alexander's Bridge* (Lincoln: The University of Nebraska Press, 1977). Used by permission of the University of Nebraska Press.

Colette, *Cheri* and *The Last of Cheri* (New York: Farrar, Straus and Giroux, 1951). Used by permission of Martin Secker and Warburg, Ltd., and Farrar, Straus and Giroux, Inc.

Colette, "Break of Day," in *Gigi and Selected Writings* (New York: Signet, 1963). Used by permission Martin Secker and Warburg, Ltd., and Farrar, Straus and Giroux, Inc.

Dass, Ram, and Mirabai Bush, *Compassion in Action* (New York: Harmony Books, 1992). Used by permission of Crown Publishers, Inc.

de Beauvoir, Simone, *The Second Sex,* translated and edited by H. M. Parshley (New York: Alfred A. Knopf, 1953). Used by permission of Random House, Inc.

Dew, Robb Forman, *Fortunate Lives* (New York: William Morrow, 1992). Used by permission of William Morrow and Company, Inc.

Drabble, Margaret, *The Garrick Year* (London: Weidenfeld and Nicolson, 1964). Used by permission of Weidenfeld and Nicholson.

Eliot, George, *Silas Marner* (London: Macmillan, 1913).

Eliot, T. S., *The Cocktail Party* (London: Faber and Faber, 1949). Excerpt from *The Cocktail Party* copyright 1950 by T. S. Eliot and renewed 1978 by Esme Valerie Eliot, reprinted by permission of Harcourt, Brace and Jovanovich, Inc., and Faber and Faber Ltd.

Ephron, Nora, *Heartburn* (New York: Alfred A. Knopf, 1983). Used by permission of Random House, Inc.

Fitzgerald, Zelda, letter to Scott, in *Zelda Fitzgerald: A Biography,* by Nancy Mitford (London: The Bodley Head, 1970). Reprinted by permission of the Bodley Head and the estate of the author.

Flagg, Fannie, *Fried Green Tomatoes at the Whistle Stop Café* (New York: McGraw Hill, 1988). Used by permission of Random House, Inc.

Gilman, Charlotte Perkins, *The Home: Its Work and Influences* (Urbana: University of Illinois Press, 1972).

Gould, Lois, *Such Good Friends* (New York: Random House, 1970). Used by permission of Random House, Inc.

Hawes, Elizabeth, *Anything But Love* (New York: Holt, Rinehart and Winston, Inc., 1948). Copyright 1948, © 1976 by Elizabeth Hawes. Reprinted by permission of Henry Holt and Company, Inc.

Heilbrun, Carolyn G., *Reinventing Womanhood* (New York: W. W. Norton, 1979). Used by permission of W. W. Norton and Company.

Horney, Karen, *Our Inner Conflicts* (New York: W. W. Norton, 1945). Used by permission of W. W. Norton and Company.

Howard, Jane, *A Different Woman* (New York: Dutton, 1973). ©1973, 1982 by Jane Howard. Used by permission of the publisher, Dutton, an imprint of New American Library, a division of Penguin Books U.S.A., Inc.

Lessing, Doris, "Between Men," in *A Man and Two Women* (London: MacGibbon & Kee, 1963). Copyright © 1963 by Doris Lessing. Reprinted by permission of Jonathan Clowes, Ltd., London, on behalf of Doris Lessing.

Luce, Clare Boothe, quoted in the *Bulletin of the Baldwin School*, September 1974.

Lurie, Alison, *Love and Friendship* (New York: The Macmillan Company, 1962). Used by permission of Macmillan Publishing Company.

Mansfield, Katherine, "Frau Fischer," in *In a German Pension* (London: Penguin Books, 1975).

Marshall, Paula, "Reena," in *Reena and Other Stories*, published by The Feminist Press, © Paula Marshall, 1983. Reprinted by permission of the author.

Matthau, Carol, *Among the Porcupines* (New York: Turtle Bay Books, 1992). Used by permission of Random House, Inc.

Moodie, Susanna, *Life in the Clearings, Versus the Bush* (Toronto: McClelland and Stewart, 1989).

Morrison, Toni, *Sula* (New York: Alfred A. Knopf, 1973). Used by permission of the author.

Pilcher, Rosamunde, *The Shell Seekers* (New York: St. Martin's Press, 1987). Copyright © 1987 by Rosamunde Pilcher. Reprinted with the permission of St. Martin's Press.

Plath, Aurelia Schober, *Letters Home: Correspondence, 1950–1963* (New York: Harper and Row, 1975). Reprinted by permission of HarperCollins, Publishers.

Rich, Adrienne, *Of Woman Born* (New York: W. W. Norton, 1976). Used by permission of W. W. Norton and Company.

Richardson, Dorothy, *Pilgrimage* (New York: Alfred A. Knopf, 1967). Used by permission of Random House, Inc.

Sand, George, *Intimate Journal*, in *Revelations: Diaries of Women*, edited by Mary Jane Moffat and Charlotte Painter (New York: Vintage Books, 1975).

Sarton, May, *Journal of a Solitude* (New York: W. W. Norton, 1977). Used by permission of W. W. Norton and Company.

Senesh, Hannah, *Her Life and Diary* (New York: Schocken Books, 1971). Used by permission of Random House, Inc.

Smart, Elizabeth, *By Grand Central Station I Sat Down and Wept* (Toronto: Popular Library, 1966). Used by permission of the author's estate.

Stanton, Elizabeth Cady, *Eighty Years and More* (New York: Schocken Books, 1971).

Steinem, Gloria, *Revolution from Within* (Boston: Little, Brown, 1992). Copyright © 1992 by Gloria Steinem. By permission of Little, Brown and Company.

Tweedie, Jill, *In the Name of Love: Love in Theory and Practice Throughout the Ages* (New York: Pantheon Books, 1979). Used by permission of the author.

Weldon, Faye, *Down Among the Women* (London: William Heinemann, 1971). Used by permission of William Heinemann, Ltd.